As new doors of opportunity open before you, I encourage you to walk through them. Be bold in pursuit of your passion. Be smart in the ways you execute your plans. Be creative in the journey so that your light shines bright. Be courageous in your daily endeavors and be confident that you are designing your own life as it was intended.

Be.Inspired. Be.Empowered.
Touch the Sky!

Sincerely Yours,

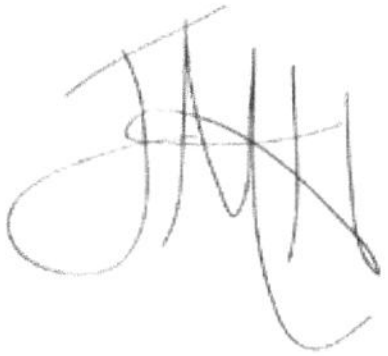

www.juliemholloway.com

www.twitter.com/jmhcre8ive